□ RANGE
GRASSHOPPER
SPARROW

□ RANGE
BALD EAGLE

HONEYCREEPER

Hawaii

□ RANGE
SPOTTED OWL

□ RANGE
KIRTLAND'S
WARBLER

□ RANGE
FLORIDA
SCRUBJAY

THE BAHAMAS

A PLACE FOR
BIRDS

For Vicky Holifield, whose incredible
editorial vision first saw the potential
in my picture book manuscripts.

—M. S.

This is for Countess and Fred
Metcalf. Their love, care, and
kindness gave me wings.

—H. B.

Published by
PEACHTREE PUBLISHERS
1700 Chattahoochee Avenue
Atlanta, Georgia 30318-2112
www.peachtree-online.com

Text © 2009, 2015 by Melissa Stewart
Illustrations © 2009, 2015 by Higgins Bond

Book design by Loraine M. Joyner
Composition by Melanie McMahon Ives
Illustrations created in acrylic on cold press illustration board.
Title typeset in Hardlyworthit; main text typeset in Monotype's Century
Schoolbook with Optima initial capitals. Sidebars typeset in Optima.

Printed in November 2014 by Imago in Singapore
10 9 8 7 6 5 4 3 2 1 (hardcover)
10 9 8 7 6 5 4 3 2 1 (trade paperback)
Revised edition

Library of Congress Cataloging-in-Publication Data
Stewart, Melissa.
  A place for birds / written by Melissa Stewart ; illustrated by
Higgins Bond.
      p. cm.
  ISBN 978-1-56145-839-4 (hardcover)
  ISBN 978-1-56145-840-0 (trade paperback)
  1. Birds—Juvenile literature. 2. Birds—Effect of human beings
on—Juvenile literature. 3. Birds—Effect of habitat modification
on—Juvenile literature. I. Bond, Higgins, ill. II. Title.
  QL676.2.S7527 2009
  598—dc22
                                             2008036744

A PLACE FOR
BIRDS

Written by
Melissa Stewart

Illustrated by
Higgins Bond

PEACHTREE
ATLANTA

Birds fill our world with bright colors and sweet songs.
But sometimes people do things that make it hard for them
to live and grow.

If we work together to help these amazing winged creatures, there will always be a place for birds.

FEATHERS AND FLIGHT

A bird's most exceptional feature is its feathers. They help a bird stay warm and dry, hide from enemies, and attract mates. Most important of all, feathers help a bird fly. Air flows smoothly over a bird's wing feathers. A bird uses its tail feathers to steer, slow down, and keep its balance.

Great blue heron adult and chicks

Like all living things, birds need safe places to raise their young. Many birds lay their eggs close to the ocean.

PIPING PLOVER

Piping plovers lay their eggs on beaches. Because the eggs and chicks blend in with their sandy surroundings, sunbathers and joggers may step on them by accident. In the late 1980s, people began fencing off some beach areas while the little birds raise their young. By 2010, the plover population had begun to recover.

When people set aside and protect parts of the beach,
birds can live and grow.

Some birds can only build their nests in small hollow places.

When people build nesting boxes that are the right size and shape, birds can live and grow.

EASTERN BLUEBIRD

Eastern bluebirds used to nest inside dead trees and rotten fence posts. But over the years, people cut down dead trees on their land, and farmers replaced wooden fences with metal ones. Luckily, bird-watchers noticed the problem. They began building nest boxes for bluebirds, and the effort paid off. Bluebirds have made an amazing comeback.

Many birds need to build their nests in wide open fields.

GRASSHOPPER SPARROW

In the past, small farms with open fields covered much of New England. But in the last few decades, people have built houses and shopping malls on the land. Scientists at Westover Air Reserve Base in Chicopee, Massachusetts, wanted to create new places for grasshopper sparrows and other grassland birds to live. They set aside 1,500 acres of land and mow the area just once a year. That gives the birds plenty of space and time to lay their eggs and raise their young.

When people create new grassy areas, birds can live and grow.

Even when birds build their nests in safe places, their chicks may not survive. If adult birds eat food full of poisonous chemicals, they may not be able to lay healthy eggs.

When people stop using these dangerous chemicals, birds can live and grow.

Bald Eagle

In the 1940s, farmers began using DDT to kill the insects eating their crops. Some of the poison flowed into rivers and streams and entered the bodies of fish. When eagles ate the fish, the eggs they laid had weak shells and their chicks died. By 1963, only 400 pairs of eagles lived in the wild in the continental United States. Many people worked hard to outlaw DDT. In 1973, they were successful. Today more than 9,000 nesting pairs of bald eagles live in the continental United States.

Adult birds face many dangers too. Some birds have trouble surviving when new animals invade the areas where they live.

When people stop animals from spreading into new areas
and work together to get rid of the unwanted invaders,
native birds can live and grow.

CRESTED HONEYCREEPER

Early settlers
brought farm
animals to Hawaii.
Some of them
escaped into the
wild and bred in
large numbers.
Over time, goats ate
many rain forest plants. Pigs tore
up native plants as they rooted
through the soil. Crested honeycreepers began to have trouble
finding enough flower nectar to
eat. But concerned people took
action. They built fences to
keep pigs and goats out of
the places where crested
honeycreepers live.

HERMIT THRUSH

Every autumn, millions of birds fly south in search of warmer weather and more food. In the spring, they return to their northern homes to mate and raise young. Because hermit thrushes use the stars to navigate, they often fly toward city lights and crash into tall buildings. In 1995, skyscrapers in Chicago, Illinois, began turning off or dimming their lights while birds are migrating. This policy saves more than 10,000 birds each year. It also saves energy.

autumn. Bright city lights can confuse these migrating birds and cause them to crash into buildings.

When building owners turn off lights at night during the migration season, birds can live and grow.

Migrating birds can be confused by windows too.

ANNA'S HUMMINGBIRD

Each year, at least 365 million birds die after crashing into windows in the United States. Migrating birds, such as Anna's hummingbirds, are at the greatest risk. The birds are fooled by windows that reflect trees or bushes. They may also crash if they can see through a window to a window on an opposite wall. You can help these birds by adding images to your windows or by using window blinds or shades.

When people mark their windows or pull down shades, birds
can live and grow.

Birds that eat seeds don't have to migrate. But if they go to backyard birdfeeders, they may be attacked by a hungry housecat.

When people keep their pet cats indoors,
birds can live and grow.

NORTHERN CARDINAL

Cats are hunters. Their natural instincts tell them to attack anything that moves, including cardinals and other birds. Peter Marra, a scientist at the Smithsonian Conservation Biology Institute in Washington, D.C., estimates that cats kill as many as 3.7 billion birds every year in the United States. Keeping pet cats indoors can save cardinals, chickadees, and other birds that visit backyard feeders.

Birds have trouble surviving when their natural homes are destroyed. Some birds can only live in thick woodlands with lots of large, old trees.

SPOTTED OWL

During the last 150 years, more than 80 percent of the old-growth forests in the western United States have been cut down. If the logging continues, the forests—and the creatures living there—will soon be gone. In 2008, a large area of land in Arizona, Utah, Colorado, and New Mexico was set aside to help protect one group of spotted owls. Now scientists are hoping the birds will be able to survive.

When people protect the land and the trees,
birds can live and grow.

Other birds can only survive in open woodlands with small, young trees.

When people work to restore these wild places,
birds can live and grow.

KIRTLAND'S WARBLER

Kirtland's warblers depend on young jack pine trees and the grasses growing below them for food and nesting spots. Long ago, natural wildfires regularly burned the land. But when people settled in the area, they started putting out the fires. By 1987, Kirtland's warblers were almost extinct. But recent efforts to create new habitat for Kirtland's warblers are really paying off. The little bird is well on its way to recovery.

Many birds live on land that is perfect for building homes and growing crops.

FLORIDA SCRUB JAY

The dry, sandy scrubland that Florida scrub jays call home is easy to clear and build on. It's also ideal for growing orange and grapefruit trees. As a result, Florida scrub jays are losing land at an alarming rate. When students at the Pelican Island Elementary School in Sebastian, Florida, learned that these birds were in trouble, they sprang to action. In five years, they raised enough money to buy twenty acres of scrubland near their school.

When people protect these natural areas, birds can live and grow.

When too many birds die, other living things may also have trouble surviving.

PLANTS NEED BIRDS

Many birds eat berries and other fruits. The seeds inside the fruit aren't harmed as they pass through a bird's body. When the bird releases its wastes, the seeds land on the ground. If the soil is rich and moist, the seeds will grow into new plants. Many plants depend on birds to carry their seeds to new places.

That's why it's so important to protect birds
and the places they live.

OTHER ANIMALS NEED BIRDS

Birds are an important part of the food chain. Eggs and chicks are good sources of food for raccoons, snakes, lizards, foxes, coyotes, mink, weasels, skunks, and snapping turtles. Adult birds are often eaten by foxes, coyotes, weasels, badgers, mink, and larger birds. Without birds, many other creatures would go hungry.

Birds are the modern relatives of dinosaurs. They have lived on Earth for about 150 million years.

HELPING BIRDS

❖ Keep your cat indoors.

❖ If your home or school has windows that might confuse birds, mark them or use window blinds or shades.

❖ Do not spray chemicals that could hurt birds.

❖ Join a birdwatching group in your area.

❖ Start a wildlife garden in your yard or neighborhood.

❖ Ask your parents to buy duck stamps. Consider entering the Junior Duck Stamp competition.

Sometimes people do things that can harm birds. But there are many ways you can help these beautiful winged creatures live far into the future.

HELPING BIRDS HELPS US

Wildlife gardens can provide birds with everything they need to survive. To get started, you'll need a water supply and a variety of plants. Some plants should provide cover for the birds. Others should produce berries or seeds for the birds to eat. The workers at a local garden center can help you choose plants that will grow well in your area. Besides enjoying the beauty of birds and other creatures, you'll probably notice fewer annoying insects. Some birds can eat a thousand mosquitoes in a single afternoon.

Bird Facts

* No one knows exactly how many kinds of birds live on Earth. So far, scientists have discovered more than 10,000 different species.

* All birds lay eggs. Bird nests come in a wide variety of shapes and sizes.

* Many birds migrate in the spring and fall. The tiny arctic tern travels about 22,000 miles from its summer home to its winter home.

* Birds do not have teeth. They use beaks to grab and tear apart food.

* Scientists think that birds developed from small meat-eating dinosaurs.

Selected Bibliography

Attenborough, David. The Life of Birds. Princeton, NJ: Princeton University Press, 1998.

Milius, Susan. "Cats Claim Billions of Bird and Small Animal Victims Annually." Science News, February 23, 2013, p. 14.

_____. "Windows Are Major Bird Killers." Science News, March 22, 2014, pp. 8–9.

Sibley, David Allen. The Sibley Guide to Bird Life and Behavior. New York: Knopf, 2009.

U.S. Fish and Wildlife Service. 2011. "Abundance and Productivity Estimates–2010 Update: Atlantic Coast Piping Plover population." Sudbury, Massachusetts.

Acknowledgments

The author wishes to thank Doug and Jessica Stewart for photos of their bluebird nest boxes and Natural Resources Manager Drew Milroy for allowing her to tour the grassland conservation area at Westover Air Reserve Base in Chicopee, Massachusetts. Phil Huber, Wildlife Biologist, Huron-Mainstee National Forest's Ranger Station, Mio, Michigan; Doug Stotz, Conservation Ecologist, Field Museum, Chicago, Illinois; and Bonnie Swanson, former principal, Pelican Elementary School, Sebastian, Florida, took time out of their busy schedules to discuss projects that are protecting birds and preserving their habitats.

Recommended for Young Readers

Alderfer, Jonathan. National Geographic Kids Bird Guide of North America. Washington, D.C. National Geographic Society, 2013.

Aston, Dianna Hutts. An Egg is Quiet. San Francisco, CA: Chronicle Books, 2006.

Henkes, Kevin. Birds. New York: Greenwillow, 2009.

Stewart, Melissa. Feathers: Not Just for Flying. Watertown, MA: Charlesbridge, 2014.

Stockdale, Susan. Bring on the Birds. Atlanta, GA: Peachtree Publishers, 2011.

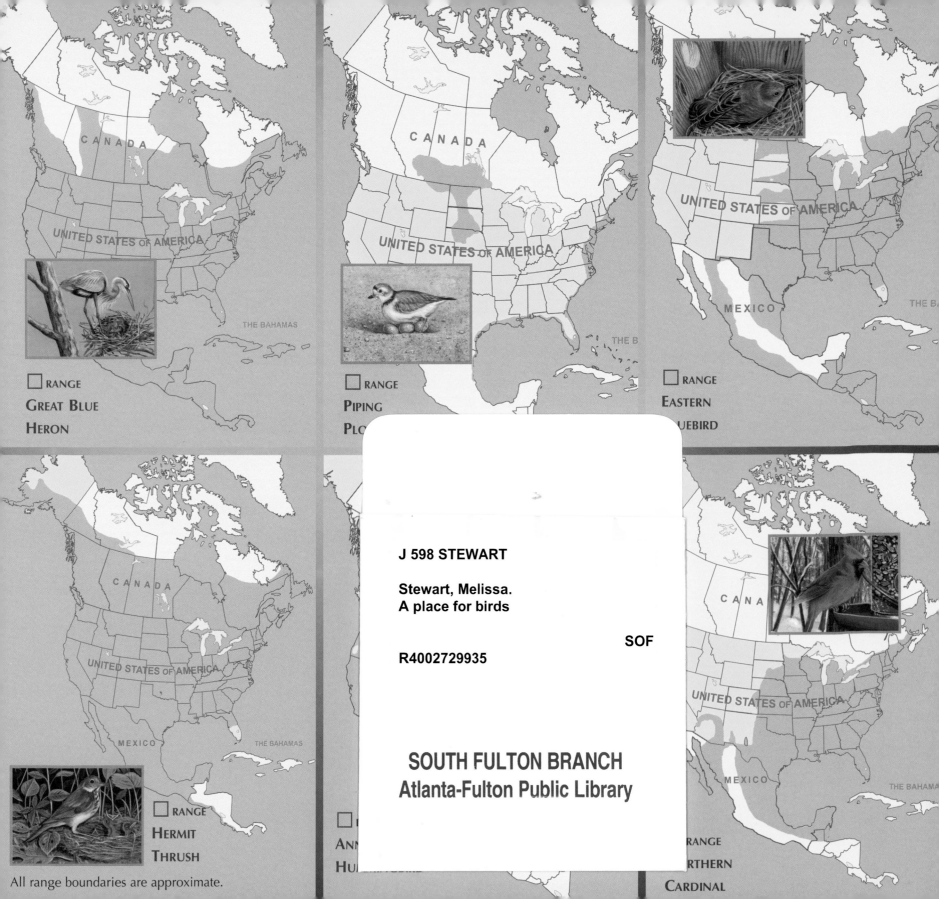

☐ RANGE

GREAT BLUE
HERON

☐ RANGE

PIPING
PLOVER

☐ RANGE

EASTERN
BLUEBIRD

☐ RANGE

HERMIT
THRUSH

All range boundaries are approximate.

☐ RANGE

ANNA'S
HUMMINGBIRD

☐ RANGE

NORTHERN
CARDINAL